50 INDUSTRY SECRETS:
WHAT I WISH SOMEONE TOLD ME BEFORE I GOT INTO REAL ESTATE

 ••••••••••••••••••••

Written By:
Sherell S. Robinson, BS, AA, CTSP

Dedication:
To my heartbeats, my girls- Ibby & Illy.
To my ummi, who told me to "just do it already."
To pop pop, Dewight. Every step you took...every field you worked...from Georgia to Philly...your life was a gift to me.

Author's Note

A perfect book for:
Real estate agents
Landlords
Small and large real estate developers (flippers etc)
Aspiring homeowners
Lenders
Family and friends of real estate agents
Real estate wholesalers

This is a no-holds-bar collection of tips, moments of enlightenment, resources and hard truths that can impact those finding their way in real estate, as agents, everyday folks, and even those who come into contact with real estate pros and aficionados all over the world. A newfound light is shone on this prominent, fast growing and important industry.

After reading this book, **agents** *can identify that it takes more than real estate courses, paid fees and completed state board exam to be great in their* *field. This book is the golden goose for real estate agents to learn what others may never share with them to increase industry success. On the other side,* **brokers** *who read this book can connect better with the experience of their independent contractors. The* **public** *and others who come into contact with agents can learn what their agent is responsible for, what they endure, and how they can help agents help THEM!*

Real estate **investors** *can gain insight about what they can expect while working in certain areas of the industry. The everyday, curious person can also identify solutions to issues you are likely to face or may already be facing in real estate.*

Those who work with individuals in the real estate industry can identify how to make their job easier, experiences better, and possibly create better business, and relationships in real estate.

●●●●●●●●●●●●●●●●●●●●●●

Above each tip/truth you will find who primarily could relate to what is presented. This is done for those of you who may only want to skim information that you feel is specific to your role or proximity to the real estate industry. If you are not a real estate agent, please do not be offput by the fact that I specifically address real estate agents in much of the information shared in the book. I still want you to read EVERY tip/truth because you never know which sentence will be the gem that you or someone you know needs on a given day!

TABLE OF CONTENTS

11 | One: Letting Your License Expire Or Sit with The State Too Long Can End Everything!

12 | Two: Get a Goal & Activity Book

13 | Three: You Need a Motivation Plan That You'll Use Daily

15 | Four: You Need a Self-Care Plan That You'll Use Daily

16 | Five: Checklist Overload Is Key

18 | Six: Prospects Will Lie About Their Plans to Give You Their Business

23 | Seven: Your Ultimate Priority Is Not a Broker's Ultimate Priority

24 | Eight: Are You With a Parent-Friendly or Balanced Work-Life Type of Agency?

26 | Nine: What You Look Like Matters

29 | Ten: (Sort of) Read Everything BEFORE You Need It

30 | Eleven: You Need to Have Savings

34 | Twelve: You Have to Wait Longer Than Corporate Folks to Get Paid

36 | Thirteen: You Need To Know Your UVP Going In

42 | Fourteen: Don't Try To Mirror Other Agents

43 | Fifteen: You Don't Need to Be Associated With a Big Name Broker

45 | Sixteen: You Don't Need to Be Associated With a Big Name Broker

46 | Seventeen: Your Fellow Agents Are Not Above Discriminating

49 | Eighteen: Your Fellow Agents Are Not Above Discriminating

51 | Nineteen: You Don't NEED To Be a Realtor

55 | Twenty: A Criminal Charge Can Impact Your Ability to Practice

59 | Twenty One: Having No Affiliation with a Broker Impacts Your Ability to Practice

60 | Twenty Two: Your Knowledge Must Go Beyond Real Estate Itself

61 | Twenty Three: Your Broker Aint Cho Mama!

62 | Twenty Four: Your Family & Friends May Not Choose You to Rep Them

63 | Twenty Five: Some Of the Most Extensive Work You Do Won't Involve Compensation

65 | Twenty Six: Niching Down is Only Pseudo-Real

67 | Twenty Seven: It Isn't As Fancy As It Seems

69 | Twenty Eight: Uncle Sam WILL Come Knocking

70 | Twenty Nine: Some Leads Won't Be Converted For Months Or Even Years

71 | Thirty: You Need to Specialize In Connecting & Communicating

72 | Thirty One: Safety Has to Be a Top Priority

74 | Thirty Two: You Can Get Money by Tapping Other Markets Even With a License From One State

76 | Thirty Three: Oftentimes You're Not Making Money Because Of You

79 | Thirty Four: Clients Put the Onus On You...Even With What is THEIR Responsibility

81 | Thirty Five: You Will Be Disrespected

82 | Thirty Six: It's Electrifying When You Know What You're Doing

84 | Thirty Seven: Asking For Business Doesn't Have to Be a Production

84 | Thirty Eight: You Should About Care About E&O

85 | Thirty Nine: Those Events You Ignore Revive Your Motivation

86 | Forty: Your Social Pages Matter

89 | Forty One: You May Feel Forever Tethered to the Field

Black Agent Section:

91 | Forty Two: You Will Be Triggered A LOT

92 | Forty Three: …And You STILL Belong

93 | Forty Four: You Must Learn To Separate Opinions From Truth

94 | Forty Five: You Need a Toolkit For Surviving Repeated Microaggressions

95 | Forty Six: You'll Experience Steering That May Not Seem Like Steering on The Surface

98 | Forty Seven: You Are a Unicorn

99 | Forty Eight: The Industry Was Not Originally Made to Include People Like You & Your BIPOC Clients

100 | Forty Nine: You'll Be Asked to Make Concessions That Non-Black Agents Are Not Asked to Make

102 | Fifty: The Industry is No Better or Worse Than Other Industries in Many Ways

agents – landlords – developers
1. <u>Letting Your License Expire or Sit with The State Too Long Can End Everything!</u>

The timeframe for keeping an expired or inactive license depends on your state's relative statutes. This should have been information that you needed to know in order to pass your state exam. But if you didn't hold on to this information, simply search the statutes affiliated with your state's real estate commission. There you will find how many years you would be in the clear and at what time during your inactive period are you actually in the red zone (closer to the date that'll require you to have to retake your exam or even repeat a course!).

Developers: Any licenses and permits that you need for construction, business etc are the types of licenses that you should remain mindful of.

Landlords: Any licenses and permits that you need for business, maintaining rentals in your municipality, etc are the types of licenses that you should keep in mind.

agents – brokers - landlords – developers – aspiring homeowners

2. Get a Goal & Activity Book

This is key for your real estate dreams or current endeavors whether you're an agent, or even an aspiring property owner. You need to establish what you're working toward. Do this in a way that protects it from being a fleeting idea—here one day feeding you motivation then gone the next, when the next shiny thing from social media, or a friend's life distracts and draws you to another direction.

Agents: beyond this, a huge part of your job as a real estate agent is establishing your daily tasks which will create the results needed to meet your overall goal(s). You can only do this by concretely noting these things and tracking: 1) whether they are completed, and 2) how long that is taking. This is great for when you will also need to make adjustments as your goals, resources, and abilities change during your journey.

agents – brokers - landlords – developers – aspiring homeowners

3. *You Need a Motivation Plan That You'll Use Daily*

Work as a real estate agent, landlord, small developer etc won't be linear. Your days will include a mixture of activities. Some days will be very busy; others will not. Some days you will close deals and deposit checks. Other days you'll wonder when will you ever get a check again. As these changes occur you will face fluctuating motivation levels. Because no one sees your dream like you, you have to be your own savior. You have to be your own motivation. One key approach to being your own motivation is putting a plan in place *with tools* for when you need a push, motivation, or inspiration. My advice—get *ahead* of it! Don't wait until your motivation is *actually* depleted before you try to establish ways to push yourself further. It is better to further motivate yourself while you already have momentum going in the direction of success. It is much more difficult to push something into motion when you've already come to a complete stop AND you're the only person pushing!

I have come across some great tools for self-motivation across my career. A mentor from another industry shared that she would listen to motivational talks daily while ironing clothes, getting her children together for school, and doing odd tasks. You could even create a poster where you write daily accomplishments as they are completed from your to-do list! Seeing where we are making progress motivates us to keep going. Also, it may sound cliché—but, remind yourself of your "why" everyday. Stating your overall goal out loud each day can push you toward action. You can say something simple like: "I am making 5 contacts this evening so that I can get more comfortable networking to reach my first $1M deal. It will get done. I am already everything that I need to be to get it done."

agents – brokers - landlords – developers – aspiring homeowners

4. <u>You Need a Self-Care Plan That You'll Use Daily</u>

Agents should expect to be on-the go often. The intensity and frequency of activity can impact your health, both negatively and positively. Negatively, a busy real estate agent's schedule can lead them to forget to eat healthily and often. You could face dehydration, headaches, stomachaches, even fainting in severe cases. On the positive side, a busy agent could reap the health benefits of consistently being active and using their brain for their important work. As a part of your regimen, try having items such as snacks, ginger candies for mild stomach trouble or grumbling, OTC meds, water, a stress ball, and even a neck massager in your car.

Just as important, avoid triggers. If you have specific health issues, whether they be cardiovascular issues, hypertension, anxiety or something else, have a care management plan.

Know what you need to do to stay clear of creating severe symptoms. *Actually* carry out your prevention plan. Then have your care tools with you—like the items listed above-- just in case you start drifting into the "red-zone"! With a few care tools, you usually can recover well enough until you get back home and can rest. Flippers, landlords and others, you can benefit by doing the same as you tackle your to-do lists as well. As for aspiring homeowners—the process can be daunting. There are many moving parts a part of the process, and things also don't always come together in a snap. These are key reasons that you should heed this advice of creating your own selfcare plan and avoid triggers that you learn of as you throughout the process.

agents – brokers - landlords – developers
5. <u>Checklist Overload Is Key</u>

The best thing for an agent, broker, or other who is just starting out is to operate by checklists for various real estate processes. I don't think that it is productive to completely rely on these checklists verbatim with every single task or transaction over the long-term. If you make this a permanent habit, you may not commit the processes to memory. Think about it. Because you know that you can go in your phone and pull up someone's name to call them, how many phone numbers in your contacts have you deliberately memorized? Probably none. I know! Me too! Don't take this route with important processes in your career. Truly commit to knowing what is expected of you and the steps required for processes you will take part in. This ability can grow from starting out with checklists. But again, eventually you should feel comfortable riding without your checklist-training wheels. Also understand that checklists are used by the most experienced professionals and even institutions! So, you should not feel *guilty* if you have to use them for a time or *prefer* to use them to be sure. Just don't allow checklists to become a crutch.

agents – landlords

6. Prospects Will Lie About Their Plans to Give You Their Business

I know, horrible isn't it? What I learned that helped me avoid taking these lies personally was knowing that their lies had very little to do with my worth. In the beginning, having it done to you a number of times can make you question a lot about yourself. Although, in a sense, it could be helpful to question: "Have I made them feel that I am incapable? Was I competent and confident? What could I do to increase their faith in me to help them meet their real estate goal?"

In these cases, first, you'll feel that you don't deserve to be lied to. You'll feel resentful toward the person for having you rely on their tales for your livelihood. You'll feel that you're capable enough to carry out the tasks you're offering. So, why aren't you getting a shot? You'll feel slighted and question whether they think you're incapable of expected results. Or worse yet, you'll feel that these individuals, frankly, don't respect you. What takes these negative feelings and turns them into full blown rumination and later, a chip on your shoulder, will be the fact that this will come from your close circle of loved ones, close friends, and/or associates. In other words, this will come from people who you **expect** to support you. Ouch. That definitely makes it sting a little bit more. Also, if left unchecked, the feelings you take on will make you truly internalize that you **must** not have what it takes.

In practically all real estate trainings, or any sales trainings for that matter, you are taught to first look to your immediate sphere of influence for first sales/transactions or referrals. Your immediate sphere of influence includes the people that you see everyday and/or associate with often. These individuals are those you feel comfortable asking for their business. They are the people expected to most likely put up the least objections during the sale. They are said to sort of be your practice ground for scripts and exercising other skills to be used on bigger fish who don't know you from Adam. But, it doesn't always pan out this way. And when things don't go our way, to us, logic follows that "if my own family and friends won't support me, I must really be a joke." But the secret is, you may actually be amazing and **they** are the ones who are limited.

We're going to head down psychology lane for just a second. But, stay with me. Many of our family and friends view us only one dimensionally. This means that they only really can see us as we are in <u>their</u> lives. The role we play in their lives-- the side of our personality that they get to see are top of mind to them most of the time. In their mind, they stick us to those images with gorilla glue! So, it's hard for them to really reconfigure their mind's eye and POV of their little cousin, brother, sister, or uncle who maybe didn't get things right in the past. In some cases, they may view you as the family member who often needed their help. So, to them, you can't possibly be this new big time entrepreneur who can carry out complex real estate transactions. Uncle Todd sees you as little Lennox who used to get into tons of trouble. He doesn't credit you just yet for how much you've cleaned up your act and went after new, more meaningful ambitions. Show them. Show them by not submitting to resentment and anger. Show them a new side. Better yet, use the confidence you used to connect with strangers. Let their fears be your catalyst. That's making them work for you. And if you never get their business, so be it. I'm sure as you sat in your pre-licensing courses, or municipal office to obtain your first rental license as a landlord, you didn't hope to hedge the potential success of your whole business on them. You didn't rest everything on whether or not only people you know will bring you business. If you did assume that, you need to get back to the drawing board ASAP. But in all seriousness, change their minds eye by modeling what you *know* you are or move on.

Now, with regard to prospects who actually don't know you and lie about plans for hiring you--that's easy too. They have no reference for why they should trust or work with you over someone else. This is why testimonials are great. This is also why creating repeated success can speak for you more loudly than your mouth ever could. So, put energy into those things and also practice communicating, negotiating, and recognizing and addressing objections. Prospects are just *people*. People deal in emotions then justify them with logic or closely related facts. Work that knowledge of your counterparts. You're human too, ya know? You already have the knowledge inside to succeed!

Landlords: prospects tend to worry about the many moving parts involved in renting a residence. Credit. Background checks. Bank statements. Pay stubs and more. Sharing this information with someone can feel like being exposed. Would you jump at an opportunity to expose yourself? Probably not. This could be why some individuals drag their feet until they have no other choice but to lay it all out there in the 11th hour –i.e. they really, really want to move.

Whereas, others are so resistant to feeling this anxiety or shame about, say, a bad spending or credit history, they will simply disappear back into the proverbial bushes and hope you go away.

agents -brokers

7. <u>Your Ultimate Priority Is Not a Broker's Ultimate Priority</u>

As is the case with any employer-employee (or agency-independent contractor in an agent's case) relationship, all parties involved have mutual goals and individual goals. Frankly, all of the functions that each party carry out serve as a means to an end for someone else or some entity. For you, working as a real estate agent could be a variable in an **individual goal** that leads you to an **ultimate goal**. Whereas, your agency/"employer" has employed you to carry out functions that helps them reach **their** ultimate goal. As long as the exchange is fair, beneficial to all, agreed upon and mutually consented to, it could be viewed as being advantageous.

So, **when** (not if) the time comes where it seems that you and your "employer"/agency are butting heads, take a sec to review your and their individual and ultimate goals. See whether you each are meeting in the middle to accomplish your mutual goals. Also, assess whether you, your "employer"/agency, or you both have been more focused on your own goals versus what you should be developing *together*. Where the scales of effort are tipped in the favor of one side more than the other, this is where problems usually begin to surface. Keep this in mind when you see you or your "employer"/agency becoming more irritated with the state of the results produced in your 'partnership' for mutual success. Simply work to keep balance in the picture between you two, and ask for the same in return.

agents – brokers
8. *Are You With a Parent-Friendly or Balanced Work-Life Type of Agency?*

Today's workforce is absolutely more adamant about having work-life balance. Most want work-life balance not just to be able to enjoy a family barbecue, a concert with friends, or a night of Painting With a Twist. Many individuals—parents or child-free—may want flex time to do other meaningful paid work. Some also like using free time to volunteer for charitable causes. Most of us care about whether we make it home with energy to make memories with our children, or other loved ones, before our day is done.

Regarding parenthood--although fewer people are having children these days, it is obviously still taking place. Also, there are plenty of already existing children of people in today's workforce. Because of this, employers/agencies have to take into account that their workforce includes parents who have a genuine interest in actually being parents. This also means people do not want to give all of their days to work. This means that people want security and certainty. They don't want their work circumstances to repeatedly feel threatened, unstable, or in limbo over the term of their career with an employer. If you feel this way, don't dismiss these desires and rights. Take a look at your brokerage or brokerage of interest and determine whether they measure up to this.

I have always worked with agencies that seemed very parent-friendly. Children could get in even on the marketing! Or, if an agent needs to make some quick copies or drop off an escrow check, we were allowed to have our little one tag along. But remember, workplaces are not childcare facilities. Know your children and whether or not it is a bad idea for them to accompany you to the office. A bored child can be a little volatile. So assess your child's willpower and likely tendencies to decide what's realistically best.

agents
9. *What You Look Like Matters*
I am not speaking to ethnicity and such here. I am speaking to overall presentation of self. This includes how you adorn yourself, your hygiene, the orderliness of your physical presentation and the like. All of which speaks for us to those whom

we are engaging with. And what our presentation says about us, to others, will be different depending on the purpose of the interaction. As much as possible, we must be cognizant about what our presentation says about us throughout important career moments—such as while trying to be hired by a prospect!

For instance, if someone engages us to see if we will be a good fit as a childcare provider, they are looking for cues that (in **their** mind) represent qualities specific to the role. In our physicality they are looking for cues that signal to them what they want to know about us. This is because they don't have much else to go off of. These cues or symbols are what show up via the clothing we choose, how orderly we appear etc. They are usually very subjective. So don't define those cues literally, or how **you** would view them. Putting yourself in the mind-state of the prospect is the only view that matters in many instances, like when you're trying to earn someone's business. For instance, in a childcare provider, one would be looking for someone who appears to be warm, reliable, friendly, competent and even fun. The symbols or cues that may convey this to the person assessing us could include: a cozy cardigan, fun colored eyeglasses, quality brand clothing, tucked in, tied, or buckled in an orderly manner. Obviously, someone could wear all of these items and be the opposite of the qualities mentioned. But, humans don't always follow logic. Instead, we lazily rely on cues, and short cut information like our own limited visual references—such as what someone's clothes convey about them. Still, the adage: "dress the part" is not advised frivolously. I say this because it is advised based on proven psychological concepts such as use of authority symbols like a suit. If you want to read more about this concept and how you could ethically use it to your advantage in business, check out the renowned book called "Influence: the psychology of persuasion" by Robert B. Cialdini, PhD.

agents – brokers - landlords – developers – aspiring home owner

10. (Sort of) Read Everything BEFORE You Need It

Working as a real estate agent can create anxious feelings, since at the beginning there seems to be so much that we need to learn. This is why it pays to begin reading relevant materials, infographics, how-tos, office boilerplate and more, long before you need it. For instance, agents-- even if you have no buyer clients just yet, this does not mean that you have unlimited free time to make pretty or aesthetic social media posts. While it is important to cultivate your social media presence, it is important to almost always be getting more and more familiar with the day-to-day information and materials that are crucial to doing your **actual** job as an agent.

This would involve reading over different contracts/agreements. Don't just read buyer agreements. Read over listing contracts, rental agreements, addendums a landlord-client may need, such as a pet addendum and more. Learn what title documents look like. You should also note that what you need to read and become familiar with does not stop at specific real estate documents. You should be doing the same thing with books and materials that can inform you of best practices for communicating with clients, presenting ideas clearly, how to gather the right information from a client and so forth.

Everyone who isn't an agent: it pays to become familiar with processes you have a stake in. Consult relative Youtube or Tiktok videos, magazines, industry and organization newsletters, non-fiction books, relative textbooks and more to familiarize yourself with your real estate interests and other important information.

agents – brokers - landlords – developers – aspiring home owner

11. You Need to Have Savings

Generally, a real estate agent does not have consistent dependable dates by which they can expect to have long term, consistent, dependable paychecks. An agent could create something reminiscent of consistent paychecks by establishing a pipeline of deals. This pipeline will establish something like an assembly line of closing dates. Only then will an agent be able to expect a check cut by their broker. Staggering deals is difficult because no one can guarantee a real estate transaction that occurs exactly by expected schedule. Deals will almost never progress based on the scheduled timeline intended by all parties in a deal. Things happen!

Like any other person saving for their responsibilities, one needs money for rent, utilities, daily meals, possibly medication, daily toiletries, required and elected insurances, creature comforts such as entertainment and more. For example, even if you're going to a free park, you need money to get there. This is just the tip of the iceberg if you have children or a dependent whom you provide and care for.

The most common business expenses for an agent would be:
- Equipment
- necessary subscriptions (dropbox, docusign, MLS etc)
- signs & riders
- postcards
- business cards
- social media ads
- gas
- car maintenance
- client gifts
- open house materials
- ink ink and more ink
- paper
- printer
- laptop and/or tablet
- postage
- self-care (this is NOT an option

a street team unless you yourself and family or friends distribute doorhangers, flyers or postcards throughout your farm (service) area.

*Note: farm area- area that an agent services through their real estate

MLS-Multiple Listing System, region specific database where licensed agents and brokers list and search area properties, retrieve market data and use agent tools like customer relationship management (CRM) systems.

Landlords: Even if you have a property manager, you will need funds for the parts of the business that you still have practical involvement in. For instance, having a basic printer, computer and such will be among your expenses. Furthermore, you are a property owner. There is no doubt you should have savings for future maintenance and other relative costs.

Aspiring homeowners: you should have savings for closing costs (usually 3%-4% of the home's price). You should also have savings for maintenance and bills that may come about after closing on the property. Surprise costs can tank a homeowner's finances, more so, if they haven't planned ahead.

Developers: savings are mainly kept by you guys for contingency funds needed during construction and other parts of your building journey. It should be accounted for in your pro forma if you're developing more formally.

agents – brokers – developers
12. You Have to Wait Longer Than Corporate Folks to Get Paid

When we get paid as agents is always a hot topic among newer or inexperienced agents in our real estate circles. There are no reliable weekly or bi-weekly payments waiting for real estate agents. Our performance and the status of our transactions determine when our pay day comes, and how much. Generally, the only way to escape this volatile wage schedule is to have enough deals in one's pipeline that when one contract closes, we can expect our next payday upon the closing of the next deal up for settlement (or a signed lease if you are a leasing agent or landlord).

When it comes to how much, by law, the percentage of the rent or sales price paid to an agent is always negotiated between an agent and client. However, an agent generally receives 3% of the transaction property's sale price. Or in cases of a lease, an agent generally receives 50%-100% of the amount of one month's rent. Given recent commission split case rulings, it's imperative that you consult NAR's website and/or government sites for more detailed information about how new laws will affect you/your role in real estate.

Also, don't forget that a check is issued when a deal is closed. But, your brokerage will need time to subtract their fees or portion of your commission. **Then** your pay is dispersed to you. My point is-- the payment process isn't as simple as someone hiring you and you receiving a Cash App. There is a process and this is why having some savings, gig work or other avenues for earnings in this career can be an important consideration.

Developers: we often see our payday extremely further down the road because many projects simply break even. As a result, we are left waiting for the property to turn a full profit before we get back our investment in full or start to see profit from rents, miscellaneous income etc.

agents – brokers - landlords – developers – aspiring home owner

13. You Need To Know Your UVP Going In
UVP-Unique Value Proposition

I won't spend too much time defining and explaining this concept. Primarily, you should know that it is key to all of your marketing and professional communication as an agent, broker, or agent.

If you don't know your UVP going in, you will waste many months and years as a real estate agent, putting out weak marketing messages to the wrong targets. Also, when you don't identify what is special about you, you may feel inclined to chase what every other agent is doing versus what would work best for accomplishing <u>your</u> professional goals with your prospects ideal for the real estate lane that you are in.

Your UVP is that thing that makes you different from everyone else. As a real estate agent, we are speaking to the unique skillset that you have and how to make it of use in your role as an agent. Your uniqueness is formed by your particular professional and personal experiences, along with **any** education you've acquired. No, you didn't have to graduate college and be in the top 3%. And I don't care if your education solely consists of math and history courses from high school before your pre-licensing courses! Use those strengths! For example, you could use your strong suit in memorization and interest in history by soaking up historical info about properties that you show, or by remembering cool facts about your client's interests. Use your strong suit in general math by impressing your clients with getting their numbers right in a deal every time! Use your great memory and knack for gift giving by utilizing what you remember about client hobbies and continuing fun and unique or creative closing day gifts. To succeed in real estate, you don't have to be anyone else. Just be you! It WILL set you apart in the overflowing sea of real estate agents who show up as your competition.

As stated, we all need to know our UVP because it is the foundation that all of your marketing campaigns, marketing materials such as flyers and social media posts etc will be built upon. Knowing why you are unique to work with as a real estate agent and noting this uniqueness in social posts, while networking, and more can ensure success.

An example of a unique value proposition: Lauren came from a childcare background and has a knack for creating fun experiences. In her new life as a real estate agent, she needs to identify

education and skills that she has used in the work noted above that can be applied. After taking inventory of her background, she notes that she:
- connects well with children
- easily reassures parents
- is safety oriented
- Can make diverse individuals feel welcome
- Can stay calm in high emotion situations
- Creates fun experiences and environments

Let's break down how these skills are transferable to her role as a real estate agent.

Work In Childcare	How to put it to use as an agent
Connects well with children	Her niche becomes: 'aiding those with finding homes for families w/ children'
Easily reassures parents	Uses property knowledge, neighborhood info, local school knowledge etc to address family concerns and highlight how conducive the neighborhood and local

	resources are to each family.
Is safety oriented	Identify sources of danger and how specific homes and features counter that danger. She also easily communicates how that is helpful to the family and their children.
Can make diverse individuals feel welcome	Expands how many families she can actually help as an agent.
Can stay calm in high emotion situations	Address inevitable issues in real estate deals with ease and pass on that calm demeanor to nervous clients
Creates fun experiences and environments	Creates fun, family-oriented open houses and networking events to expand her professional reach

Considering this chart of Lauren's transferable skills, we could say that Lauren's UVP (unique value proposition) is that she is: ***"The family's agent"* with exclusive knowledge of markets and locales fit for every family.**

Developers: Knowing what is different about you as a developer is key to what you highlight in marketing. It is also key to identifying who you should target as end users of your project/property. For instance, if you do sustainability and placemaking well, you know that you should target individual or investor buyers or tenants who can appreciate those specific elements. Then once those targets are identified, you can tailor your marketing to draw them to your property which you know they'll love.

Aspiring homeowners: What is unique about you as a buyer can be key to positioning yourself in a way that best communicates to a seller why you should be the winner in the offer wars for their property!

agents
14. Don't Try To Mirror Other Agents
It may be tempting to follow tons of other agents on social media. It is just as tempting to copy marketing campaigns that said agents roll out to drum up new clients and attention. However, their goals and skillset are all their own. Therefore, nothing that another agent is doing should be done to the T. This would be like following someone else's recipe to produce a signature taste that <u>you</u> imagine. Your efforts have to truly come from and be designed by you. Sure, it is fine to identify general methods that work. But, you have to put yourself out into the stratosphere. That won't happen if you're a knock-off/2.0 version of another agent.

agents

15. You Don't Need to Be Associated With a Big Name Broker

FOMO (fear of missing out) is the leading cause of thinking that you must only be associated with prestigious or well known names/agencies to succeed. Many newbie agents (and others honestly) fear that if they don't sign with a big name, they will not have access to desired clients, resources and opportunities. What if I told you that according to a NAR poll reported by the Tampa Bay Times, only between 3%-4% of buyers and sellers care about the particular agency that a real estate agent is associated with?

In my own experience, I have been associated with, both, larger national real estate brands and mom and pop level real estate agencies. My main take aways are this:

In larger agencies: A pro of reputable, bigger name firms is that they are not too difficult to be hired by. But, I got lost in the sauce. I was not paired with more experienced agents as I had hoped, because the office needed them to be out being the agency's shining stars. I yearned for more substantive and impactful in-house training. If any training was given, it was very general, regurgitated new agent advice. I was left on my own to "figure it out". I was also required to do "floor time"—answer incoming calls and walk in prospects in specific time slots on specific days. This was not compensated time. I was let go from one big brokerage as soon as I had trouble maintaining enough deals and savings to cover E&O insurance and affiliation with a Realtor Association and connecting local chamber. I felt compelled to reconnect with a big name because bigger names are more easily recognized by prospects. In some cases, individuals will assign success to you simply because you are associated with the bigger names. I had to recognize that lead conversion still wasn't guaranteed.

In mom & pop agencies: Mentors and answers to questions—even in the 11th hour—were very easily accessed. Training was exceptionally plentiful and even very nuanced. I never attended trainings that seemed as if I was repeating general info from a pre-licensing course to appear busy. I was not required, but had an option, to complete some floor time. I was not required to join a Realtor Association. I did not need to carry expensive E&O insurance. The broker did so. Also when deals were not as plentiful and I had trouble covering costs with license renewal, continued education, obtaining signage, lockboxes or otherwise, I was provided various options for assistance. I also had access to the office whenever I chose to be there.

agents – brokers - landlords – developers – aspiring homeowner

16. It Is Okay to Not Be On 24/7

We typically adopt the idea that we should be contributing to our career, our goals, giving to our clients, and closing deals every minute of every waking hour in a day. Most of us agents got into real estate due to the available schedule flexibility. Some of us liked the idea of dabbling in other work, scheduling time with family more consistently and the like. If that is why you chose a career in real estate, then don't begin thinking that you should turn over your life in a way that other agents may. Maintain your own goals, your own balance in life. But, do remember that your pay, completed professional tasks (agents and other professionals), and completion of your goals (aspiring homeowners) are in direct proportion to what you dedicate of yourself. Just be sure to create balance between all of this.

agents – brokers
17. You Should Choose a Diverse Brokerage
When choosing what brokerage to be affiliated with, an agent is best served by choosing a diverse agency. An agent can best serve their brokerage and the public at large by choosing to be a part of a diverse brokerage.

A brokerage should be diverse ethnically and experientially. An agency that is diverse ethnically is able to expand its reach. Different individuals who live different lifestyles would be able to experience accommodation by your agency if it happens to be diverse. From this comes the opportunity to serve a more widespread customer base. This isn't just a strategy to make an agency lucrative. It makes for a cultured, expansive, and interesting career experience for everyone in the agency who gets to come into contact with individuals that come from different walks of life. Furthermore, working in a diverse brokerage creates an additional means of connecting and collaborating with colleagues. If you and a fellow colleague have a need for what one another has to offer, say, in terms of opposite experience or another language, you're able to aid one another. This positively impacts morale at the agency. But even more, this familiarity and comfort with someone previously considered different can translate out of the office into societal communities. As people feel less disconnected from lifestyles, cultures and individuals different from them, gaps within the human family come together a bit more, little by little.

In opposition, strictly sticking to what is like you closes you into a restricted world. You lose access to all of the things mentioned above. Losing access to more clients, more connections, and the opportunity to help create a better society should be enough reason to avoid non-diverse brokerages. But beyond this, only sticking to what you know and only what you are comfortable with, restricts the 'harvest' that you provide to your family and/or self. Obtaining limited knowledge, limited experiences, limited professional reach, limited connections means you model, teach and provide for those in your sphere by a meager provision. Don't you want to give to your children, parents, friends and others abundantly? This is not possible by living in a limiting way.

agents – brokers
18. Your Fellow Agents Are Not Above Discriminating

I know that we like to believe that any circles that we choose to become a part of are –for the most part--wholly good inside and out. However, we neglect to remember that institutions, establishments, and other places that we become a part of include humans! Humans come with all sorts of conditioning, subconscious beliefs, biases, and generally different ways of looking at life matters and other people. Because of this, the real estate industry is not exempt from including these kinds of people just like any other industry.

So we're all on the same accord, I'll start this off simply. I'll define exactly what I am speaking of in this section. By definition, according to Merriam-Webster, discrimination is "prejudiced or prejudicial outlook, action or treatment."

As an African American, visibly Muslim, female, I have seen my fair share of discrimination. Based on zero facts, I have had a broker tell me that I was not producing deals because I wear garb. He was referring to my hijab. Garb would actually reference full body attire, which I did not wear at the time. I wore suits! I have encountered male agents who would completely ignore and/or interrupt me everytime that I would speak during property meetings. They would avoid even offering eye contact for practically the entire 45 minute- 1 hr meeting. One interaction included one male agent almost solely speaking to the other male in the room, who was **MY** client. I can also recall an incident where I walked up a driveway to visit a property in place of another agent. I got a long stare through the window. Before I knew it, the half opened door was slammed closed before I approached. I don't think I have enough pages to even cover what all I have experienced while putting in offers for clients. Implicit and overt discrimination live in that area of real estate work as well!

I have a host of these experiences, but I think that you get the picture. The point is, if you feel it and it is based on your gut and circumstances, do not rule out that you have been treated unfairly. It is possible and you should not gaslight yourself about your experiences. Most of us have lived enough life to recognize when we are treated less than fair. Trust that and take the proper steps to buffer these inevitably horrible moments. But, also do your individual best to avoid being a part of this pool of tainted agents, builders etc, or crying wolf at every instance of misunderstanding.

agents
19. You Don't NEED To Be a Realtor©
It's important to preface my elaboration in this section with quick definitions so we're all on the same page. All Realtors are real estate agents. But not all real estate agents are Realtors.
I know some reading this are thinking: "What?! I thought a real estate agent and Realtor were the same thing!" Kinda sorta. Let me elaborate.

A real estate agent takes the appropriate pre-licensing courses required by their state that the agent will practice in. This qualifies the candidate to sit for the state board test that their state requires to become a licensed real estate salesperson. Once this is accomplished, the newly licensed person links with a brokerage/company in order to act in a real estate agent capacity. A real estate salesperson is an independent contractor loosely supervised by a broker—the person leading the brokerage/umbrella company. An agent reports their own taxes to the IRS upon making earnings. Agents do not receive a W-2. But rather, they receive a 1099 form from their broker. If an agent so chooses, they can submit a request to be a part of the National Association of Realtors and accept its code of ethics. To maintain membership with the association, an agent must pay monetary dues, continue education, abide by restrictive use of the "Realtor" trademark and more. Having experienced being a non-Realtor agent and a Realtor, the main difference was costs and the permission to use the word Realtor on marketing materials. All else, to me, bears no substantive difference.

Particularly, NAR requires (at the time of this writing) a $156 dues fee every month. In addition, a Realtor would also pay the state license renewal fee every two years and Continued Education costs required by their licensing state. Some brokerages may offer free continued education. In such cases, that is the opportunity to save on recurring career expenses.

Furthermore, NAR requires Realtors to abide by their code of ethics. Some believe that this makes Realtors stand out in ethics in morality. However, there are ethics practices that must be known and adhered to even for a non-Realtor to obtain and keep their status as an agent. Something to also take into account is that ethics and morality can only exist in a person who has this as part of their basic personality foundation. Ethics and morality cannot be trained into someone, no matter who is providing the training. So, although it is admirable that NAR requires this to be a part of their board, one should not discount that these things naturally come from within and are already required to become a licensed non-Realtor in the first place.

Additionally, NAR members (Realtors) are given the opportunity to pay for designations. Designations issued by the National Association of Realtors are titles that a Realtor can display having paid the appropriate fee and completed the relative training. For instance, some designations could identify an international real estate specialty, buyer specialty, commercial real estate specialist or otherwise. I would note that a non-Realtor can obtain credentials as well through education at local colleges. However, designations obtained by Realtors are specialized credentials to the board. Whereas, credentials obtained through colleges could be widely accepted beyond the real estate world and tend to be actual degrees or accredited certifications. Obviously, an agent considering additional education and credentials will want to identify if those from colleges are credit bearing programs or non-credit. One should also consider how much NAR and college credentials/titles mean to them and their sector of the industry.

*Note: Some real estate brokerages require agents to maintain status as Realtors in order to maintain employment there. I didn't know this when I once practiced real estate at a large New Jersey brokerage. I was "let go" when I couldn't pay Association fees anymore as shared previously.

agents

20. A Criminal Charge Can Impact Your Ability to Practice

A background check and fingerprinting are both conducted during the preliminary process of becoming a real estate agent. This is how someone wanting to become a real estate agent must be cognizant of their criminal history. One should also be mindful of whether minor matters can be expunged off of their record. Overall, there must be consideration of whether you have the character strengths and habits necessary to uphold the duties and privileges of serving the public as a real estate agent for the long haul.

Why would it be important to know if a person trying to work in the real estate industry has a criminal history or propensity to commit crime? There are possibly 101 reasons why this is important, but there are a few that stick out to me most prominently.

Real estate agents have access to lots of sensitive information. Clients provide business information and records. They provide social security numbers, bank information and addresses too. Criminals with a propensity to fraud, preying on unsuspecting or trusting individuals could wreak havoc on a client whose information that agent is able to access. Essentially, an agent has access to information that could allow them or a criminal associate to even assume their client's identity!

Protecting clients from this level of betrayal is important and hence, is part of why criminal backgrounds are conducted.

Real estate agents have access to a person's primary sense of security, the families of others, and a big chunk of the net worth of others—their property. People create a home to solidify a place in the world that is their own. A home is a person's retreat and that of their family. The net worth of the average property owner is predominately carried by the property that they own. Having access to all of these things gives an agent the ability to impact these areas of a person's life. Essentially, an agent can impact a client's quality of life and that of their family. Being in such a position, clients must be protected from unscrupulous individuals who may seek to become licensed agents and have access to this power.

Brokers need to know who is under their roof. It is important for a broker to know the behavioral track record of a newly hired agent. Agents are representative of a broker and his or her agency, and what that agency represents. Because of this, a broker will be generally concerned with how a prospective agent of the agency generally acts. Also, in the case of liability, what an agent does, his or her broker can be on the hook for legally, financially, and otherwise.

Only allowing behaviorally sound people into a profession adds credibility to the field. Where a field has some exclusivity, as to the character of those who are a part of it, that field is supportable. It is noble of the profession itself to be proactive in protecting those who will be served by relative professionals. Whereas, if the industry did not have a standard of who can do what while working as a licensee, the industry would likely be avoided. Having customers avoid an industry reliant on customer relations and customer trust would be a dying industry. So, this is also why it is important for the industry to corroborate whether its professionals are only those with favorable character.

agents
21. *<u>Having No Affiliation with a Broker Impacts Your Ability to Practice</u>*

States require that licensed agents work under the supervision of a broker for the entirety of the life of their license activation, and while operating in the capacity of a licensee. Therefore, when an agent decides they do not want to be affiliated with a broker, they are required to temporarily retire or deactivate their license to their department of state. As long as the license is up to date with renewal fees and such, the license will remain in good standing. But the agent is not allowed to work in an agent capacity and receive commissions. You usually steer clear of any complications as long as you reactivate the license and join a brokerage before the license actually expires. If your license has been inactive or expired up to a certain amount of time (in PA it is five years)-- you're required to repeat the licensing exam for the state in which you would like to practice.

The other route one could take is to just become a broker themselves. Each state has requirements for qualifying to sit for the state's broker's licensing exam. Check with your state's real estate commission to determine the number of credit hours in the broker's pre-licensing course. Then check for the documents needed in order to sit for the exam. Completing this would enable you to avoid having to worry about being under the "umbrella" of a broker with just a real estate salesperson license.

agents – brokers - landlords – developers
22. *Your Knowledge Must Go Beyond Real Estate Itself*

It is helpful to increase your knowledge of the following:

- communication
- interviewing

- motivation
- psychology of influence
- credit repair
- creating feel good atmospheres
- psychology of buying
- micro and macro markets
- recourse for worst case scenarios
- legal timelines
- The U.S. History (or your area's historic backdrop) of the industry & your position

agents
23. Your Broker Aint Cho Mama!
Brokers are not in the business of handholding. They want agents to make money for them and contribute to a positive reputation for the agency. They also want an agent to contribute to the agency's ability to meet overarching goals. They will always provide some sort of resource Motivate yourself! Get your own leads. Introduce yourself, reach out for help on your own.

agents

24. Your Family & Friends May Not Choose You to Rep Them

I know. This looks similar to the section about how prospects will lie to you about their "intention" to give you their business. But, this section is a little more nuanced, although in a similar vein.

This section isn't about your immediate circle of influence lying about what they intend to do. This is about that close circle of family, friends and associates outright choosing someone else over you to do exactly what your job is. This is done without them ever stating whether they would or not.

This becomes problematic when you felt **entitled** to the business/support of your family or friends when they had a need that you could fulfill and create a livelihood from. But instead, your family and friends selected someone else to represent their interest. You will likely feel all of the troublesome emotions noted in a previous section. But, my advice is to prevent at least some of those emotions by lowering your expectations of your family and friends. Don't **expect** their business. Try and **earn** it as you would with anyone else. Also, understand that the reason that you were chosen over by your friends and family may have to do with the reasons noted in the similar section above. Therefore, you should follow those solutions as well.

agents

25. *Some Of the Most Extensive Work You Do Won't Involve Compensation*

Real estate agents are not highly paid tour guides. We create, maintain and revive complex processes that contribute to the net worth of individuals, families and even communities. This entails:

- Finding, cultivating and managing leads
- Maintaining market knowledge DAILY

- Developing contracts, researching and analyzing data
- Maintaining trustworthiness (possessing private information and funds)
- Managing attitudes involved in transactions
- Managing resources and contacts (title companies, lawyers, contractors, notary etc)
- Negotiating, scheduling, event planning (open houses), facilitating showings
- Serving as client therapist and advocate
- Chauffering clients
- Staging, housekeeping and being handyman/woman and much more

Because we orchestrate processes with so many moving parts, there are small and large tasks that we <u>must</u> complete in order for a deal to move forward. As a result, every sweat that we break is not compensated. Granted, it is possible to have colleagues, say, facilitate a showing or open house for us. However, to create a streamlined experience of consistent quality and expectation for our clients, we should maintain order over our own transactions. We can do this by keeping our own finger on the pulse of our deal. Generally, our commission is paid at the conclusion of a deal for everything, large and small, that we have done to bring the deal together. When we have worked with a client for two years in the buying process, or done everything possible and the deal still dies, we go through these instances unpaid. Consult your savings and self-motivation tools to get through these tough moments! Also, use your discernment to determine whether these tough circumstances outweigh any success you are having overall. If the bad far outweighs the good, it is time to assess your efforts, review the types of deals and prospects you've been landing, ask for help and assess whether it is time to consider other opportunities.

agents – developers
26. Niching Down is Only Pseudo-Real
Real estate agents are very often told to niche down and find a professional sweet spot where

we will gear our efforts. This could mean deciding whether we want to solely work in commercial real estate or strictly residential, and strictly do rentals or buyers and sellers. Then being even more nuanced would involve breaking either of those categories down further. For instance, we could choose to work in commercial real estate, and particularly work with larger scale retail real estate or condo buildings.

The reason that I say niching down only seems pseudo possible is because many of us learn that we will end up playing in another pond when leads dry up in one area. Also, many areas of real estate seem to overlap.

> Example: *Sarah decides that she wants to sell commercial retail. She learns that commercial retail real estate involves long close dates (and pay dates). So, she decides that it is important to garner new leads that may close more easily and quickly. With these thoughts she decides to take on commercial residential real estate clients. In this area she hopes to work with sales specifically.*

However, as she works with clients, they are often asking her to also work with them to get the units leased. Her Commercial retail clients have asked the same. Here, Sarah thought that she would strictly stick to commercial sales, but ends up moving into rental territory as well, although still in the commercial sector.

agents – brokers - landlords – developers – aspiring homeowners – loved ones of agents

27. It Isn't As Fancy As It Seems

What comes to mind when you hear the title "real estate agent"? Someone in a suit, fancy shoes, leather work bag, someone carrying an arm-full of papers on a cell stepping into a luxury car, maybe? An Instagram image of an agent holding a sold sign or a client holding a check. Agents popping champagne and being recorded in slow motion walking up the walkway of a luxury home? Yeah, so does mostly everyone else. Maybe one of these descriptions was the mental image that made you pursue this role in the first place. Either way, if you've started working in real estate already, those images have likely gone up in a puff of smoke.

The reality of the work of a real estate agent is tedious, almost constant and requires adding lots of consistent drops in a bucket to reach a substantial end result. This hard work doesn't happen without sweat, some doubt and a few tears. You will be asked questions you don't know the answer to. You will have someone lose their s*** for something that has nothing to do with you. You will begin your celebration with a client on a deal and in the 11th hour, the other party will want to back out. You will need to be at a meeting, but look in your bank account and see that you're $4 short for the uber you need RIGHT now. This is the picture that many start with in their real estate career. But, others start off just fine, or either end up just fine. You can decide what your picture looks like.

agents – brokers - landlords – developers – aspiring homeowner

28. Uncle Sam WILL Come Knocking

You are deemed an independent contractor while you are working as a real estate agent. And as an independent contractor, you are responsible for a number of things and that includes paying taxes on your earnings. For agents, it is very important to put the adequate amounts aside with cashed checks, so that you can pay your taxes. Otherwise, when you file taxes, you will have a balloon bill and the IRS will do everything in its power to reap the owed amount from you. For agents, even if years later you take up work in another capacity, future checks can be garnished, as can settlements and more.

Landlords and developers: as you know, your taxes are inevitable as is the case with agents. It is important to note that your tax considerations are more extensive than those of a real estate agent or broker given that you have property and unique business variables related to your taxes.

Aspiring homeowners: When you consider funds needed over time to pay your mortgage, also consider that your real estate taxes must be paid every year. Also, note that local tax assessments can drastically change for any number of reasons (gentrification etc). Therefore, it is important to heed previous advice about having adequate savings for things like this.

agents – brokers - landlords – developers
29. Some Leads Won't Be Converted For Months Or Even Years

I know you think you read that wrong. Nope. It's true. Real estate deals come about as a result of cultivated relationships. Cultivating relationships and building rapport takes time. So, the time between when you first meet someone and the moment that you sign a lease or reach the settlement table may include months or years. It is not uncommon to hear an agent mention that they've worked with a buyer for more than a year. With buyers specifically, they go through so many emotions throughout the process. They can be excited and motivated early on. They then can experience doubt and fear as the process hits a few bumps. This may lead them to pause the home search for months—by ghosting or giving notice. You may begin showings again and finally submit offers and complete the process. This could add an extra 45 days. Real estate processes are not linear and neither are the emotions of humans. So, prepare yourself for this mentally and by managing resources to help you help your clients in these moments!

agents – brokers - landlords – developers
30. You Need to Specialize In Connecting & Communicating

As stated in multiple sections, you need to connect with individuals in order to pull real estate transactions together and to get clients. Therefore, without connecting and knowing how to communicate with others properly, you will not have a real estate career. Watch videos and read books about communicating and connecting for professional success in general.

agents - landlords

31. Safety Has to Be a Top Priority

Unsavory individuals are constantly looking for opportunities to swindle, steal or even harm individuals when an easy opportunity presents itself. With the amount of personal information that agents have of others—escrow checks, credit card numbers, social security numbers with addresses and birthdates, bank information, investment files, deeds—a criminal could have a field day. In addition, we are often contacted for meet-ups and showings by complete strangers. We encounter strangers while conducting open houses. This should not be taken lightly—especially depending on your locale and what crime norms exist there. Consider some of the following tips to be proactive with protecting yourself and to react best should you find yourself in danger.

1. Do a quick internet search of individuals who reach out to meet up with you.
2. Identify whether a prospect knows anyone mutually, so that you can get a live reference of their personality.
3. Have someone join you on appointments and at open houses
4. Carry key-ring alarms and even pepper spray
5. Don't place yourself in extremely exclusive quarters with anyone when you are alone
6. Arrive early and survey immediate surroundings
7. Mentally create a loose safety plan for exiting a home in multiple ways
8. Let others know where you will be, with whom, and even share your location
9. Possibly live stream portions of the open house and make others aware that you will be doing so. Unscrupulous people likely won't want to go on camera.

10. Incentivize people you are meeting or who plan to attend an open house to register basic identifiable information before attending. You could even make it fun or let them know that they can receive access to some intangible giveaway or other property tour if they sign up.

agents – brokers – landlords - developers
32. <u>You Can Get Money by Tapping Other Markets Even With a License From One State</u>

This section is not telling you to function as an agent in other states where you are not licensed. But rather, interstate partnerships are key to carrying out a plan for tapping into markets in other states. This may be where being part of a larger brokerage will truly come in handy. In larger brokerages with multiple locations—in different states—there are agents to whom you can refer prospects. Simply charge a referral fee to the agent. Do some quick research to determine the average referral fee in your area AND ask your broker what is typical. Compare the information that you receive. Also, don't forget to put the matter to your broker as a beneficial option that will leave no money on the table for you both. Share how many prospects come to you looking for real estate services for a particular state. Let them know that you won't limit the money that you bring in simply because you have a real estate license from one state. But, you WILL do everything legally! Reassure him that you understand the importance of liability prevention. You cannot become so engrossed in landing deals that you begin drifting into the shadier end of the deal pool. Stay on the right side of the line and ask questions if you come across anything that makes you pause. Do not swim out into unknown territory in a blindfold.

Landlords and developers: You can connect with agents and brokers of different locales to get your properties rented or sold.

agents - landlords

33. Oftentimes You're Not Making Money Because Of You

Bet that bit you a little bit. I even cringe when I read it. I know that this has been true for me and is true for me in moments where I slip into a coasting mode. It is very easy to feel for a moment that you can rest on your laurels and coast for juuuust a little bit. You justify your inaction by noting how much you deserve to rest. Although, it really isn't about rest. Instead, it's really about fear, some ignorance, and habits. You tell yourself that your pipeline is rolling and that it's fine if you hold off on adding anyone else to it. You crazily convince yourself that you can get away with avoiding networking this week, or not calling that guy who's interested in grabbing a property to flip. These are the tasks that are the beginning of bull-splitting (you know what word I want to use instead).

As mentioned, a former broker told me that I wasn't selling homes because I wore "garb". In reality, aside from the fact that I didn't have a mentor in him doing his best to support me, I wasn't attending to the little tasks that led me to big deals. I wasn't seeking those who didn't know that they needed me and what I could provide. In the days of flyers—I wasn't creating them and getting them out to the *correct* target prospects. I did not have a consistent plan that I worked daily to bring in leads. I did not put in enough effort to convert leads. I let prospects drive the boat. I did not face their objections with pre-practiced and proven to work responses. I wasn't educated on the emotional process that prospects go through. So, I wasn't identifying where they were in that process so that I could meet them there with everything that they needed to move toward with becoming my client. I was not putting myself out there, so that everyone everywhere in my specialty area knew that I was around to assist them. All of these things and more were well within my capability. But, I didn't know that they were things that I should have been doing to get myself the volume of contacts and business that I desired and needed. Don't be me. Know these things (and more) and act on them...immediately. Get a mentor and talk to your broker often about what you should be doing right now to produce results for you both.

Landlords: consider the marketing you are choosing to use to find quality tenants. Also consider the condition of the property that you are offering. Does it speak to the type of tenant that you are seeking? Are too many areas outdated? Consider your communication style. Are you asking offputting or legally discriminatory questions? For instance, are you hyperfocused on keeping out tenants who have a small child whom you assume will damage your property? Consider whether you make it difficult or easy for tenants to see your home or complete the application as a tenant. All of these things and more could be factors that are creating obstacles to reaching your financial goals.

agents – aspiring homeowner

34. Clients Put the Onus On You...Even With What is THEIR Responsibility

Being placed on a learning curve for anything really is nerve wracking at some point. This goes for all humans. So, when working with clients remember that they are humans. Therefore, this applies to them as well. They hired you because you know 1) what they don't and/or 2) can do what they can't or won't do. Therefore, even with things that they can and/or must do themselves, some will try to get you to do it. Be prepared to face this. Sit down with a mentor or your broker to have a brainstorm session with all of the in-house agents. Have them create a list of typical tasks that clients may usually try to pawn off onto the agent. Then you guys can list scripts, resources, or general ways to re-direct your client in these moments. Next, you'll need to work on your confidence, willpower, and tact. These three things will be key in helping you pause your client's buck-passing attempts. They will help you feel empowered to respectfully reject their demand you can then give them other options for getting their needs met without overloading you, or creating the wrong expectation of your role and willingness. You must establish the tone that will be followed in your single transaction, as well as **all** of your future transactions to come. Furthermore, remember that what you practice is how you condition yourself to function on auto-pilot. If you practice being a wuss, doormat, yes-man/yes-woman who constantly takes on work that is not yours, all while you are not being paid, you will never be happy in your career. There is no pride in being spineless for the sake of POSSIBLY receiving a dollar at the end.

Aspiring homeowners, family and friends of agents: don't be this client.

agents – brokers – loved ones of agents
35. <u>You Will Be Disrespected</u>

By clients, colleagues, brokers, and any of the professionals that you interface with alike. This has little affect on you where you establish how you expect to be treated. You establish this by how you carry yourself and also by reiterating it in cases where it seems to have been lost on someone. As they say, "let 'em know!". Now, the ways in which this comes about? Take your pick. You may be disrespected by someone refusing to hear your input. You may be dismissed when you bring up something that is important to you. As shared, I have had doors slammed in my face where prejudice was involved. You will be ghosted by other agents whom you have put offers in with. I have been yelled at by clients, who were actually upset with their lender's requests. A broker once asked me questions about the religion that I follow. He shared how his and mine had similarities and differences. He went on about the concept of prayer. He noted that, in all but words, he told another agent who possibly follows the same religion that I do, that he doesn't acknowledge her prayers because " I know where **my** prayers are going. I don't know where the hell **yours** are going!" There are so many ways that disrespect can play out, because why you guys? Say it with me—we're dealing with humans! Stay human—along the better part of the human spectrum. And it will make your experiences easier even when they are hard—such as being treated with varying levels of disrespect.

agents – developers
36. It's Electrifying When You Know What You're Doing

I feel electric like chills running through me right now as I think about the moments that have created this feeling for me! Listen, I know that when you are first starting out, or even when you have some experience under your belt in real estate, your nerves take a beating constantly. Look, if you look on my Tiktok page-- @realestate..rell—you'll see posts about "the $20,000 mistake that I made as a rookie agent".

Or, you'll see how I let a dead person pause my real estate deal due to my ignorance as a rookie agent. But, correcting those situations or pivoting those moments to better outcomes created a (good) monster in me and made those lessons gold to me and you—since I'm warning you about how not to make the same mistakes!

Simply put, continue fighting through that (with your self care and self motivation of course). This way you get to feel what its like to be on the other side. The accomplishment on the other side is unparalleled in the feeling and confidence that it creates. And guess what? Your confidence and great feelings *compound* the more that you allow yourself to reach the accomplishment at the battle. When you experience this, and you will, please shoot me an email to let me know if I was lying about how great it feels— whatiwishbook@gmail.com

agents – brokers
37. Asking For Business Doesn't Have to Be a Production

A lot of the time when we are nervous about having to do something it isn't due to the **true** nature of the thing we're nervous about. It is usually that we've made the matter **so** huge in our brains and that makes us want to run for the hills. Stop making tasks so huge in your mind! Stop catastrophizing every possible scenario. Just do it, because guess what? What happens when you do it? IT'S DONE! Literally, the act is complete and over. Like this section. Now slide to the next tip.

agents
38. You Should About Care About E&O

I briefly mentioned E & O where I shared my experience of the fees required of me while under a larger name brokerage. In a nutshell, E&O is Error and Emissions insurance that is required of a professional in case you cause ethical, financial or other damage while operating in your line of work. At some brokerages, real estate agents are required to carry this insurance. Just as with any insurance, the coverage can protect you from having to personally come out of pocket if you are found liable of something covered by the insurance. This could be helpful and also serve as a differentiator if people know that your actions are insured.

agents – landlords – developers – aspiring homeowner

39. Those Events You Ignore Revive Your Motivation

Don't push back so quickly. Trust me on this! Those free events you've been invited to, but constantly dodge actually create opportunity. That networking event you've been seeing plastered all over social media—just the same. That local entrepreneur panel that you've desperately wanted to pull together? Yup, all of them. They feel scary to address, because you're in your head about scary, **imaginary** hypotheticals. But, I can **guarantee you**, that event that you are dodging will inject something magical into your motivation tank. You're going to speak up where you didn't expect to. You will gain new insights that you can't wait to apply to your business. You'll feel the courage to plan your next business outing. And you'll feel something positive growing inside of you. You need this! Just do it and tell me about it later so that I can tell you "I told you so". 😎

Aspiring homeowners: when you are in an exhaustion-valley because you have been searching for your dream home forever, attending real estate or homeowner events can revive your zeal. This renewed spark will provide you what you need to continue strong on your search.

agents – brokers
40. <u>Your Social Pages Matter</u>

Any and all public information about you can impact what you experience in your work. Specifically, this information can impact the opportunities you gain and lose. Your interactions with other professionals and clients can be impacted based on things that these individuals have seen, read or heard on your social pages and otherwise.

Some of what we joke about, expose, share as opinions and such can offend others. We can unknowingly (and sometimes deliberately) bring harm to certain groups, certain causes and more just by putting particular ideas and behaviors out into the world. In a worst case scenario, we could offend the very person who may be essential to our business deal or some opportunity that we feel is key to reaching our goals.

We're all guilty of jumping to a conclusion or two about a stranger or even those familiar to us when we first see something pertaining to them. Self aware individuals and those with mercy correct those immediate assumptions. The next best step is to evaluate the information, evaluate the source and possibly contact the person who is the subject of the information for more clarity. But, let's be honest. Who goes through all of these steps everytime? As humans, especially in this age of a need for instant decisions, instant gratification, and a need for mental shortcuts to prevent info overload, we accept assumption as fact. Keep this in mind as you work in real estate. This is exactly what others will do when it comes to you. Google yourself. See what comes up. Scrub the internet as best you can of anything that you do not want to be misinterpreted about you as a person or professional. In addition to this, **live** out an appropriate character, so that what people see up close is real-life human goodness. And also, where you can, control what is presented in the world wide social sphere—social media. What is on your insta, Tiktok, Twitter or Youtube can be under your control. So do a good job with that presentation since there isn't much else that we can actually control. Save the full you for those who accept and deserve the full you. That does not include the general public, in my opinion.

agents

41. <u>You May Feel Forever Tethered to the Field</u>
Sometimes when you have long bouts of struggle in your real estate career, you'll contemplate "retirement". When you do, there will be a nagging resistance within that tells you to keep trying because more success or your biggest payday yet is on the horizon. This is actually a psychology phenomenon called the "sunken cost fallacy". This is the flawed thought that we should continue on with an endeavor, practice etc because we have invested so much into it thus far. Because we have invested so much time, energy etc thus far, we feel like we are on the cusp of making a break through. So, we stay with it even though it is costing us more than it may be worth. It is often the flawed thinking that causes gamblers to continue on in spite of significant losses.

Having done so much (unpaid and paid), you will feel as if being in real estate is literally an extension of your identity. This is what complicates your plans for separating from your position or the industry as a whole. When you can identify all that you are aside from work in real estate, you will be able to reconfigure an image and career that represents your new direction in life.

Consider sending past clients farewell mail. Ask them if they are open to being advised and assisted by another agent in the future (one that you trust to offer them the best). Move on with a clean break and give yourself grace as you adjust to a new schedule that doesn't include all of the "real estate" tasks you would normally be doing each day.

Black Agent Section:

EVERYONE should read this entire section just to become familiarized with the plight of fellow industry members. With these reminders or newfound insight, we can all work to create a better environment and even share tips with those whom we care about and are affected by our industry.

42. <u>You Will Be Triggered A LOT</u>

This point touches on the fact repeated here multiple times—that our industry includes humans. And as humans, we tend to see our own world first, **or only**, and this leaves us to making a lot of missteps in our dealings with others.

As a black agent, I have experienced my colleagues ignoring my calls and emails, lying about listings being inactive; along with many of the other things that everyone else goes through. However, because of the history of African Americans in our country, our common experiences in the industry will be magnified. Sometimes what we experience will be real life micro or macroaggressions. Other times, situations will be part coincidence, part ignorance on behalf of others, with other elements involved as well. To keep yourself positive and motivated, avoid gaslighting yourself about your experience. Validate what you feel. Be sure to utilize your self care plan and any support persons in your life.

43. ...And You STILL Belong

Regardless of how some individuals view you—whether their view seems justified—you are still supposed to be where you are. If you weren't you wouldn't be there. Everything in life happens purposefully. Things that exist where and how they are, do so in accordance with divine alignment. Whether this is accepted or rejected, the reality of it still plays out. So, why not hold this view as a means of helping yourself see your circumstances and yourself in a more positive light? Genuinely seeing things from a positive perspective impacts your mood and overall mindset. And your mood and mindset impact your motivation and ability to progress and achieve. See why this isn't a small thing?

44. You Must Learn To Separate Opinions From Truth

To do this, all you need to do is take a pause. Pausing creates a break in thoughts and even feelings—no matter how strong. Next, you ask yourself the right questions and start to chip away at why something is factually true or not. Doing this enough over time will make it easier and easier to discern what's factual and what is mere opinion. With this information you can less anxiously decide what matters most and move on much easier to get back to the better parts of your life.

45. _You Need a Toolkit For Surviving Repeated Microaggressions_

Being talked over and completely ignored as if you aren't in the room. Being told that discrimination you've experienced never happened and the like. Expect your experiences in the real estate industry to be an extension of what you experience in larger society. The same people in larger society, with the same limitations, and cultural incompetence find their way into the industry. So, you can expect more of the same. The main difference is that functioning in the industry involves you making a living for you and your family. And how you operate is a reflection of your level of professionalism. Therefore, you will need to exercise more restraint, consideration, and knowledge of solutions to common issues you'll face in your role. It is certainly recommended that for larger legal or basic civil rights transgressions against you, you should use all of the resources available to you. Some of these resources include:

U.S. Equal Employment Opportunity Commission
https://www.eeoc.gov/youth/filing-complaint

Professional Compliance Board for your particular state

Department of State (your state)-Licensing bureau

Your state's Association of Realtors

Directly to your state's real estate commission

46. *You'll Experience Steering That May Not Seem Like Steering on The Surface*

In a nutshell, steering in real estate is when individuals or entities in the industry deliberately direct specific racial groups, either explicitly or implicitly, to specific geographic locations. The reasons they do this is related to that individual or entity's biased views about where the steered person should be--due to their race and value position (in their mind).

What other BIPOC agents, BIPOC consumers in the real estate industry and I have experienced includes having our offers on rentals, purchases etc ignored or outright rejected based on unjustifiable factors such as stereotypes and biases. This can take place because the agent, seller, landlord, lender or whomever does not want to share commission/do business with the BIPOC agent or consumer. Or, the biased "professional" may not feel that the BIPOC consumer should live in, operate in, or otherwise integrate into the area where the property is. Or, based on biases and not on documentation etc, the individual assumes that particular groups or individuals likely aren't creditworthy, or don't have needed funds and the like.

This is not a new *concept*. It was and is used along with redlining. Much of this behavior was highlighted between the 1930's to the 1970's.

Specifically, "exclusionary zoning ordinances" were used across our United States as a means of *excluding* African Americans from middle class neighborhoods. With these regulations in place, African Americans had no choice but to predominantly settle into areas strictly amongst themselves. If African Americans managed to get into neighborhoods with Caucasians, they were evicted from properties they rightfully occupied or owned. In many cases, violence was even exacted against those who managed to settle into middle class neighborhoods that Caucasian neighbors, leaders etc did not want them to be a part of. (The Color of Law)

In addition, according to the book "The Color of Law", committees for home ownership financing would request that deed restrictions be used in conjunction with zoning restriction for added "protection" against 'black purchasing' and subsequent integration.

Need a recent reference for redlining and steering? Search for the October 2024 $6.5M settlement Citadel Federal Credit Union is required to pay!

47. *You Are a Unicorn*

In the United States, only 6% of all real estate agents are African American. (NY Times) The fact that you are here, proverbially reading about yourself as one is an anomaly. It is no small feat and you deserve to acknowledge that status. It **IS** a professional status that was initiated and accomplished by you no matter how many people try to diminish your doings in this world. Take this fact and make it worth speaking about by helping make that 6% include <u>quality</u> professionals by being one.

As stated in the above noted article, African Americans have historically been discouraged from joining the real estate profession. For instance, it was not until 1961 that the (NAR)

National Association of Realtors even let African Americans become Realtors. Up until then, they were excluded, according to the NY Times. Also, the National Association of Realtors once lobbied against legislation instituted to stop housing discrimination—The Fair Housing Act.

Aside from entering the industry as professionals, Blacks within the U.S. citizenry have also been forcibly shut out from the industry's homebuying, development, appraisal, and other sectors. This is why the simple fact that you're here is a celebratory moment. And just the same, it is incumbent upon you to make your stay in the industry impactful.

48. *The Industry Was Not Originally Made to Include People Like You & Your BIPOC Clients*

In FHA's 1934 home loan underwriting manual, neighborhoods needed to be racially segregated in order for properties to sustain their appraised value. *Some* aspects of this concept actually exist in the industry today. For instance, lenders are not legally able to use redlining maps today. But, communities with higher populations of African Americans are marked with a sort of scarlett branding. A quick google search can yield examples of how homes in these areas are less often approved for mortgage loans, and receive lower appraised values. However, if African Americans go through these processes with a Caucasian counterpart, remove their family photos etc before valuations, they receive a more favorable result. All variables controlled-- race is the only reason that could be deemed the cause for this.

49. You'll Be Asked to Make Concessions That Non-Black Agents Are Not Asked to Make

One primary reason behind this is what is discussed in the previous section. This industry was not designed to include BIPOC people! This must not be forgotten. BIPOC people were firstly not even permitted to purchase homes. From the facilitation perspective, the process wasn't designed to be permit us to guide others in real estate processes either. As a result, many individuals in and close to the field—such as old school brokers, title agents, loan officers etc—do not view our work or place in the field as noteworthy.

Beyond this, again, this field includes HUMANS. Humans come with implicit bias and worldly views of others. Some of these views hold lower regard for individuals who are a part of specific identity groups. Understand that this is the reality of our world. If someone sees you as less than—although you're not—they will attempt to deal with you in a capacity that matches that worldview of you. This could mean speaking to you in a lowly manner. It could look like them trying to convince you to accept less recognition for doing the same or more work as a counterpart who is of a different racial group. Or it could look like any of the following things:

Coaxing you to take a commission cut or no pay at all

Encouraging you to do pay-worthy things free...and often

Encouraging you to work longer hours and skimp on the balance that allows you a quality of life

Expecting you to accept disrespect, constant slights or violations and to keep quiet about them

Encouraging you to wait your turn for recognition when you deserve it now.

FINAL THOUGHTS

50. *The Industry is No Better or Worse Than Other Industries in Many Ways*

I mean, yes we have to wait a while to get paid and stay on top of continued education and license renewals. But, you have the ability to see huge paydays in relatively short periods of time, can work a flex schedule, and create a respectable career with no student loan debt. Working in real estate, in proximity to real estate, or simply owning a piece of property can all bring good to both others and ourselves. When we hire individuals in the industry, buy home improvement items and more, others are able to make a livelihood for themselves, their families, their favorite charities and otherwise. You are able to build generational wealth. We add a coin to the economy that serves us all in our country and keep it bustling. Clearly, this industry is a key to building and bolstering some of the most important aspects of life. I challenge you to remember this when you're in a valley. It should absolutely inspire you to continue to keep pushing until you arrive at your next peak! Happy wealth building!

References

"Influence: the psychology of persuasion" by Robert B. Cialdini, PhD

https://www.nar.realtor/membership/dues-information

"The Color of Law" by Richard Rothstein

https://www.justice.gov/opa/pr/justice-department-secures-over-65m-citadel-federal-credit-union-address-redlining-black-and

https://www.tampabay.com/features/homeandgarden/does-brand-matter-in-picking-real-estate-agent/2151225/

https://www.nytimes.com/2023/01/12/realestate/black-real-estate-agents-discrimination.html#:~:text=About%206%20percent%20of%20real,according%20to%20data%20and%20surveys.

Made in the USA
Middletown, DE
31 October 2024